AUDIENCE

A play in one-act

by

Michael Frayn

SAMUEL FRENCH, INC.
45 WEST 25th STREET   NEW YORK 10010
7623 SUNSET BOULEVARD   HOLLYWOOD 90046
LONDON   *TORONTO*

IMPORTANT BILLING AND CREDIT REQUIREMENTS

All producers of AUDIENCE *must* give credit to the Author of the Play in all programs distributed in connection with performances of the Play and in all instances in which the title of the Play appears for purposes of advertising, publicizing or otherwise exploiting the Play and/or a production. The name of the Author *must* also appear on a separate line, on which no other name appears, immediately following the title, and *must* appear in size of type not less than fifty percent the size of the title type.

AUDIENCE was first presented in *Colin Blakely, a Celebration,* at the Lyric Theatre, London, on October 4, 1987. With a second act added, it was presented under the title *Look Look* by Michael Codron at the Aldwych Theatre, London, on April 17, 1990, with the following cast:

AMANDA ....Serena Gordon
CHARLES .... Michael Simkins
BOBBIE.......................................Joyce Grant
MERRILL...................................Ken Wynn
HELENA .... Gabrielle Drake
JOAN .... Margaret Courtenay
QUENTIN.............................. Robin Bailey
LEE................................ Steven Mackintosh
KEITH...................................... Stephen Fry
REGINALD.............................John Arthur
EILEEN.......................................Pat Keen
WENDY ....Lisa Jacobs
USHERETTE..................... Jeanne Mockford

Stage Manager ....Krissy Wilson

Directed by ....Mike Ockrent
Designed by .... Carl Toms
Lighting by ....David Hersey

CHARACTERS

F 13 (JOAN)
F 14 (HELENA)
G 12 (QUENTIN)
G 13 (LEE)
G 14 - later G 15 (WENDY)
G 15 - later F 15 (CHARLES)
G 15 - later G 14 (REGINALD)
G 16 - later F 16 (AMANDA)
G 16 (EILEEN)
H 18 (KEITH)
I 16 (BOBBIE)
I 17 (MERRILL)
USHERETTE

AUDIENCE

A proscenium arch, seen from behind. The tabs are in. They are in fact a scrim, and in the last few minutes before the start of the play the lights behind them gradually come up to reveal, rather dimly, a kind of mirror image of the auditorium, with members of an audience being shown to their seats by an usherette, buying programmes, taking off their coats, and chatting.

All that can be seen of this second auditorium, in fact, is a section of the stalls, with one of the aisles and the entrance doors at the back. Twelve seats are defined in various parts of the central block: four side by side in the row nearest the front (Row F); five side by side in the row behind (Row G); one, way off to one side, in the row behind that (Row H); and two side by side in the backmost row (Row I). [See illustration #1 on page 48.]

By the time the play starts nine members of the audience have taken their places in these thirteen seats.

In I 16 and I 17, at the back, an American couple: BOBBIE, in her fifties and in command, and MERRILL, in his seventies and no longer in command of anything much, not even his faculties.

In H 18 - KEITH, in his forties and wearing seedily casual clothes.

In G 12 - QUENTIN, who is in his fifties and knows everything about the theatre. Beside him, in G 13 -

7

LEE, who is in his late teens and knows nothing about anything.

In G 15 - CHARLES, a middle-aged man being remarkably attentive to his companion, AMANDA, in G 16, who looks as if she is being hunted by the police.

In F 13 - JOAN, in her sixties, and beside her in F 14, her daughter HELENA, a distracted woman in her forties.

G 14, and F 15 and 16, remain unoccupied.

The USHERETTE has taken her place by the double doors at the back.

[See illustration #2 on page 49.]

MUSIC. The USHERETTE closes the doors. The houselights begin to go down. So do the houselights on the other side of the tabs. LIGHT comes up on the tabs, until the scrim becomes once again entirely opaque. The tabs rise, revealing the audience beyond, illuminated by the spill of light from the stage they are facing, which is where we are sitting.

JOAN. (*Sotto voce to HELENA.*) ... So I told her. 'Forty pounds,' I said...

HELENA. Sh. (*SHE indicates that the curtain has gone up.*)

JOAN. (*Faces front.*) Oh, yes.

(*Pause.*)

JOAN. (*Whispers to HELENA.*) 'And that included delivery and fitting...'

(*She reluctantly abandons the conversation. Everyone stares at us in silence for some moments.*)

AMANDA. (*To herself, puzzled and irritated, in normal conversational tones and at normal conversational level.*) *Where's* this supposed to be?

JOAN. (*To herself, likewise.*) *What's* all this?

QUENTIN. (*Likewise.*) What in heaven's name ...?

BOBBIE. (*Likewise, delighted.*) It looks just so real!

CHARLES. (*Likewise.*) We *are* in the right theatre?

(*They try to read their programmes.*)

HELENA. (*Reads.*) 'Act One...'

AMANDA. (*Reads.*) 'An auditorium ...'

CHARLES. (*Reads.*) 'Evening.'

AMANDA. Oh no.

HELENA. Oh dear.

QUENTIN. God help us.

CHARLES. I thought it was a musical.

BOBBIE. I can't believe we're here! Our honeymoon—day two!

MERRILL. (*Aloud, sotto voce, to BOBBIE.*) Where's the popcorn, baby girl?

BOBBIE. (*Aloud, sotto voce, to MERRILL.*) You just hush now, baby boy.

QUENTIN. (*To himself, gloomily.*) These are supposed to be *ordinary people*, are they?

(*THEY all continue in the same manner—each speaking to himself in normal conversational tones, and each inaudible to all the others.*)

LEE. (*Suspiciously.*) These people—they're supposed to be all like symbolic or something, are they?

AMANDA. (*Darkly.*) This is supposed to be us, is it?

BOBBIE. They're so lifelike!

CHARLES. (*Gloomily.*) They look as if they've just walked in off the street.

HELENA. It all looks a bit *modern* to me.

QUENTIN. They did this in that play, what was it called, in the thirties.

CHARLES. I think this is going to be rather a yomp. Better break out the rations. (*HE offers AMANDA a box of chocolates.*)

JOAN. Well, I suppose it's the kind of thing *she* likes.

CHARLES. Seems to hold some morbid fascination for *her*, anyway.

AMANDA. (*Brushes the chocolates away.*) I read something about this somewhere. It's supposed to be all about—I don't know—something—what was it...?

CHARLES. And we might just manage twenty minutes in the car on the way back.

AMANDA. (*To herself.*) I wish they'd stop staring! I hate plays where they peer out at you. Why don't they just look at each other? We're supposed to feel got at, are we?

HELENA. It was Jane who recommended it. Of course it was Jane who recommended that one where they all took their clothes off.

JOAN. (*Thoughtfully.*) Chap there loosening his tie already.

AMANDA. They can't actually see us, can they?

MERRILL. (*Sotto voce, to BOBBIE.*) What are they saying?

BOBBIE. (*Sotto voce, to MERRILL.*) Sh!

MERRILL. What?

BOBBIE. They're not.

MERRILL. Not what?

BOBBIE. Not saying.

MERRILL. Not saying what?

BOBBIE. Not saying anything! They're thinking.

MERRILL. Thinking?

BOBBIE. Sh!

MERRILL. Thinking what?

BOBBIE. You have to work it out.

MERRILL. What?

BOBBIE. I'll tell you afterwards! Sh!

MERRILL. (*To himself.*) Thinking? We're supposed to sit here thinking 'What are they thinking?'? I know what they're thinking. They're thinking 'What the hell are *these* people thinking?'

KEITH. Funny, isn't it. You do your best to make a play relevant to the lives of the audience. You try to write about people they can identify with. What happens? Do they identify? Do they make the connection?

AMANDA. But why do they all look so actorish?

KEITH. I think they're just trying to recognise the actors.

QUENTIN. I don't recognise any of them.

LEE. They're all famous, are they? We're supposed to recognise them, are we?

QUENTIN. Oh, not *her*! She was in that thing at the whatsit.

LEE. Oh, yeah, he was in that commercial with that bloke who's in that other thing.

KEITH. Why do I have to sit here and subject myself to this humiliation? (*HE sees the empty seat in Row G.*) Oh, and an empty seat. Only been running four months, and already there's an empty seat in Row G... My God, there's two more in Row F...

QUENTIN. I'm just waiting for poor Roddy to come on.

KEITH. I'm only here because poor Roddy's off.

QUENTIN. That's the only reason I've come—to see Roddy.

KEITH. That's the only reason I've come—to see the understudy.

QUENTIN. Four months of this thing—it's a wonder he's not back in the clinic already.

KEITH. Laugh coming up here, by the way ... *Should* be a laugh here ...

MERRILL. Shut my eyes for a bit. That'll wake me up.

KEITH. No? Well, there was a laugh there. You take your eyes off a show for two minutes, and the next thing you know the theatre's half-empty and all the laughs have gone.

QUENTIN. Oh, and there's dear old what's-her-name. But what *is* the poor poppet wearing?

BOBBIE. I just love the dresses they wear.

HELENA. Ridiculous, wearing a dress like that at her age.

AMANDA. (*Shaken.*) I've got a dress like that.

JOAN. I might try that pattern in the downstairs loo .

BOBBIE. Everything taken care of. That's what I love. All the people so beautifully arranged. It's all going some place. Someone's got it all figured out.

MERRILL. (*His head jerks forward. HE opens his eyes.*) Nowhere to put your head. That's what I hate.

KEITH. I think they're beginning to settle down. Perhaps we'll get the next laugh.

MERRILL. (*Eyes closing again.*) One of these nights it's gonna roll right off.

(*People begin to stir in their seats again.*)

KEITH. No? What's worrying them now?

HELENA. I suppose there's going to be language. It's that sort of play ... I mean, *I* don't mind. I'm just worried about Mother. I know what *she* must be thinking.

JOAN. I wonder how often they have to clean that upholstery ...

QUENTIN. Anyway, it's a treat for him.

LEE. I mean, like, what's going on? Am I supposed to be *enioying* this, or what?

QUENTIN. I know how much it means to these boys to get their first taste of live theatre.

LEE. Like, why just me? I'm not the only one doing a Drama A-Level ...

QUENTIN. So valuable for them to be taken off on their own once in a while.

LEE. Soon as it's over he's going to be on about What did I think? What did I feel?

QUENTIN. Given a chance to say what they really think and feel.

LEE. I mean, how do *I* know? We haven't done this one, have we.

(*Silence.*)

KEITH. All right?

HELENA. (*Suddenly.*) What *I* resent is that there they are, all having a wonderful time swearing and taking their clothes off and sitting around as if they owned the place—and they get a great kick out of it because here we are watching them. Yet here we sit, with our clothes on and our mouths shut, and not so much as a thank you—no one taking the slightest bit of notice!

KEITH. Good. Yes. Fair point. We'll talk about it afterwards. Now ...

(*Pause.*)

MERRILL. (*Opens his eyes.*) Great stuff. When's it over?

CHARLES. They ought to put the finishing time in the programme.

(*EVERYONE shifts around again.*)

KEITH. Come on! Don't start thinking about supper.

QUENTIN. I've booked a table at that little place across the road.

CHARLES. Or if we left at the interval ...

HELENA. Could leave at the interval ...

JOAN. Go at the interval ...

HELENA. Only she won't, of course ...

JOAN. Only she paid for the tickets.

HELENA. She insisted on sitting there to the bitter end even in the one where they all took their clothes off.

JOAN. Taken his jacket off now.

CHARLES. Say eighty minutes in the car, eighty-five minutes ...

KEITH. If you're not careful there won't *be* an interval. You want an interval? You want to go home tonight? All right, then, you buckle down to it and start thinking about the next laugh. Silence. Concentrate.

(*MERRILL opens his eyes and coughs. KEITH turns round and gives him a look.*)

KEITH. Right. Thanks. Hold it. Stop there.

(*No one notices KEITH. He faces the front—and immediately MERRILL coughs again.*)

KEITH. Oh, no!

(*KEITH jumps to his feet and stares at MERRILL until he stops. But by this time CHARLES has started coughing as well. KEITH comes leaping over the backs*) *of the seats to hover behind CHARLES, unseen by anyone, as if about to murder him.)*

KEITH. You'll start them all off!

(CHARLES stops.)

KEITH. Right. That's it. No one else.

(But now LEE has started. KEITH goes leaping back to threaten him in his turn. But LEE is already acutely aware of causing a disturbance. HE stuffs a handkerchief into his mouth and shakes silently, letting no breath escape. KEITH watches over him vengefully.)

KEITH. That's right. Just suffocate in silence.

(Gradually everyone becomes aware of LEE'S sufferings, and makes great efforts not to turn round and look. KEITH watches, agonised.)

JOAN. Is someone having a fit?
KEITH. No one's having a fit.
HELENA. Is someone going to be sick?
KEITH. No, no, no! Just keep your mind on the play.
AMANDA. Someone ought to do something.
CHARLES. It's probably just one of the actors. It's that sort of play.
HELENA. Don't turn round.
QUENTIN. *(To LEE, feebly.)* All right? Better now? *(To the others.)* I don't really know this lad. He's just someone in the Drama Group.
BOBBIE. Take a deep breath.
QUENTIN. Try not to breathe.

KEITH. (*Politely.*) If you're going to die, do you think you ought to do it outside? We are only halfway through the act.

(*LEE suddenly clambers over QUENTIN and rushes out.*)

KEITH. Very sensible. Just don't ...

(*The doors slam.*)

KEITH. ... slam the doors.

(*A wild volley of coughing bursts forth outside, and echoes around the empty corridors.*)

AMANDA. Someone ought to go after him.
QUENTIN. I expect he'd like to be left in peace.
KEITH. (*HE returns to his seat.*) I knew it! Someone dying! It's that kind of audience! It's going to take another ten minutes to get them back! He's probably not even dead. We'll just have got everyone interested and he'll come creeping in again, and they'll all be listening to every move he makes, and that'll be another ten minutes gone ...

(*LEE creeps back in.*)

KEITH. He's alive. I *knew* it.

(*LEE creeps back to his place with the most careful quietness, still holding his handkerchief to his mouth. QUENTIN stands up to let him pass, looking solicitous.*)

QUENTIN. (*Whispers.*) All right?
JOAN. Is he all right?

AMANDA. Is he sure he's all right?
HELENA. He's not going to start being sick again?

(*LEE sits down. KEITH leans forwards to watch his face. Eventually LEE puts the handkerchief away.*)

LEE. OK, no one noticed, no one noticed. Just sort of hold my breath for the rest of the evening.

(*KEITH leans back in his seat. At once MERRILL takes out his handkerchief and blows a sustained voluntary on his nose. Everyone else gets out a handkerchief and starts to blow his nose, while MERRILL closes his eyes again. KEITH puts his head in his hands. When the nose-blowing at last subsides another small sound is audible—an electronic alarm watch. Everybody, except the sleeping MERRILL, gradually becomes aware of it. THEY all look uneasily round, trying to see where the sound is coming from.*)

MERRILL. Time to get up?
BOBBIE. Hush now. Back to sleep, baby boy.

(*KEITH's suspicions finally settle upon CHARLES. HE advances threateningly upon him and stands behind him. Gradually everybody else comes to the same conclusion. THEY all look sidelong at CHARLES. Gradually CHARLES realises himself, like a man in a deodorant ad who becomes aware that everyone is looking at him. Very carefully HE checks his wrist-watch. With the utmost precaution HE feels all his pockets. As careful as before not to make a noise, HE opens his briefcase and goes through its contents. Papers slip out of folders; HE retrieves them just in time. KEITH reacts to the prospects raised by the production of a mobile*)

*telephone. The cellophane wrapping from the chocolates
has to be placed silently in AMANDA's lap.)*

KEITH. I shall give you precisely ten more seconds to
get this noise stopped. Then I shall kill you. Ten seconds.

*(KEITH looks at his wrist-watch to time the ten seconds.
A terrible suspicion slowly comes to him. HE puts the
watch to his ear. HE takes it away from his ear and
touches it. The SOUND ceases. HE tiptoes back to his
seat, everyone's eyes now on him, and hides his head
behind the seat in front. Then suddenly all the other
heads snap back to watch the stage. Silence.
EVERYONE is gazing at the stage. KEITH's head
comes up sharply in surprise.)*

KEITH. What? What?
BOBBIE. *Oh* oh! Something's happening!
HELENA. *(Disgusted.)* Oh, no!
KEITH. *(Understanding.)* Oh. That.
HELENA. Sex, sex, sex.
LEE. What? Where? What's going on?
HELENA. The couple in the stalls there.
AMANDA. He's got his hand on her knee.
CHARLES. Yes, and a very conveniently placed knee
here, too.

*(HE puts his hand on AMANDA's knee. SHE does not
notice.)*

AMANDA. This is not remotely like me.
BOBBIE. This is our story.

(SHE puts a hand on MERRILL's knee. HE wakes up.)

MERRILL. Have I taken my green pill?

HELENA. *Every* time I take Mother out ...

QUENTIN. So embarrassing for *him*.

LEE. (*Interested.*) This is like that thing on the telly.

QUENTIN. I'll just have to make it up to him afterwards.

(*HE protectively pats LEE's knee.*)

HELENA. The *one* chance I get to give Mother an evening out, while Christopher's at his wildlife ...

JOAN. I wonder if those sponge fingers went down the back of the sofa.

AMANDA. Why do they keep trying to *get* at you all the time? We're not getting at them! And I have never in my life sat in a public theatre and let some man ...

(*SHE discovers the hand on her knee.*)

AMANDA. What's this?

CHARLES. What?

AMANDA. (*Takes his hand off.*) Everyone can see us.

CHARLES. Your husband can't. He's in Bonn.

AMANDA. There's bound to be people here we know.

JOAN. (*Looking at CHARLES and AMANDA.*) She's going to have melted chocolate everywhere if he's not careful.

CHARLES. (*Puts his hand back.*) They're all watching the play.

JOAN. (*Looking at CHARLES again.*) Seen him somewhere before, haven't I?

AMANDA. (*Takes his hand off.*) *You* don't seem to be watching the play.

CHARLES. I'm thinking about things. That's what you go to the theatre for—to be made to think.

AMANDA. Yes, but not to think about *that*.

CHARLES. What?

AMANDA. You know.

CHARLES. You don't know what I'm thinking about.

AMANDA. I know perfectly well what you're thinking about.

CHARLES. I'm thinking about wildlife. It's my wildlife night with Christopher Whatsit.

AMANDA. Well, don't think so loudly. Everyone'll hear.

HELENA. Why don't they ever show happily married couples going out together, like Christopher and me?

(SHE puts a fond hand on JOAN's knee.)

JOAN. *(Sotto voce, to HELENA.)* What?

HELENA. *(Sotto voce, to JOAN.)* What? *(Realises her hand is on JOAN's knee.)* Oh. *(She removes it.)*

KEITH. All right, then. Everyone alert and eager?

(MERRILL snores.)

BOBBIE. Oh, bless him!

KEITH. One missing.

(MERRILL snores again and wakes.)

MERRILL. *(Sotto voce, to BOBBIE.)* What? *(To himself.)* Where am I? Is this tonight or is this last night? OK, let's work it out. We got on the plane at nine o'clock at night. But nine o'clock at night Central Standard Time is four o'clock in the morning London time. Or is it four o'clock in the afternoon? Hey, wait a minute. This is yesterday!

KEITH. Write him off. What about the rest of them?

CHARLES. Good God! What's this?

AMANDA. (*Gazing at stage.*) What's what?

CHARLES. Another knee!

AMANDA. (*Takes his hand away.*) I was just starting to get interested ...

HELENA. (*Looking at the stage.*) The man's obsessed! Why doesn't he think about something else? Why doesn't he take up wildlife, like Christopher?

KEITH. Settle down, then, settle down. Only another page before we get to the next laugh.

(*Silence. PEOPLE are becoming interested.*)

KEITH. Good ... Well done ... (*KEITH, without being consciously noticed by the others, delicately conducts them with a rolled up newspaper towards the laugh.*) Yes. Keep coming, keep coming. We're getting there at last.

HELENA. (*Concedes.*) Quite a nice smile he's got.

CHARLES. (*Looking at the stage.*) Nice pair of knees.

JOAN. Rather nicely behaved boy.

QUENTIN. Nice bit of business with the rolled-up newspaper.

HELENA. It's just makes a nice change to come to the theatre and see some nice people behaving nicely for once.

KEITH. And ... here it comes.

(*But at that moment the doors at the back open, and the USHERETTE appears with REGINALD, his wife EILEEN, and their acutely self-conscious seventeen-year old daughter WENDY.*)

REGINALD. (*Aloud, to the USHERETTE.*) Has it started?

(*EVERYONE turns round to look.*)

EILEEN. (*Aloud.*) Sh!

REGINALD. (*Aloud, realising.*) Oh. (*Sotto voce.*) Sorry.

QUENTIN. (*To himself.*) Well, this should take our mind off things for a bit.

(*REGINALD and his family creep down the aisle behind the USHERETTE with every effort to be inconspicuous and silent.*)

KEITH. (*To himself.*) No, no! Come in! Nice to see you. We've kept a bit warm in the oven for you.

(*REGINALD and his family wait in the aisle while the USHERETTE tries to read the tickets.*)

USHERETTE. (*Mutters aloud.*) What's this, then? Q? No ... G? I don't know. I can't read in the dark.

EILEEN. (*To herself.*) I *knew* it would have started.

WENDY. (*To herself.*) Everyone staring!

BOBBIE. Oh, just look at them! Lovely happy family party.

REGINALD. I *knew* there wouldn't be anywhere to park. I told her!

EILEEN. (*To herself.*) I *knew* he wouldn't find anywhere to park. I told him!

BOBBIE. I do believe it's her birthday treat!

WENDY. Birthday? I'd rather have a funeral!

USHERETTE. (*Searching for the row.*) What did I say? Did I say F ...? Need radar for this job.

KEITH. (*Patiently.*) F? It's behind E. In front of G ...

USHERETTE. (*Sotto voce, to QUENTIN.*) You F, dear?

(QUENTIN stands up automatically, and LEE follows suit.)

KEITH. *(Patiently.)* No, he's not F. He's G.

(REGINALD and his family start to squeeze past them as inconspciously as possible.)

KEITH. *(Very patiently and quietly.)* That's Row G ... That's Row G ... That's Row G ...
QUENTIN. *(Finding the letter on the side of his seat, sotto voce.)* This is Row G.
REGINALD. This is Row G?
USHERETTE. *(Sotto voce.)* Oh, sorry, love ...

(REGINALD and his family start to squeeze back to the aisle.)

EILEEN. *(Whispers, to QUENTIN and LEE.)* Sorry ... Sorry...
REGINALD. *(Whispers, likewise.)* Do apologise ... Do apologise ...
JOAN. Why don't they sit *down*?
USHERETTE. Here you are, dear.

(SHE shows them into Row F. JOAN gets up to let them past.)

KEITH. *(Patiently and quietly.)* Programme.
REGINALD. *(Whispers.)* Excuse me ... Excuse me ...
KEITH. Programme.
EILEEN. *(Whispers.)* Sorry ... Double yellow line ...
KEITH. *(Still patiently and quietly.)* Programme.
USHERETTE. *(Whispers.)* Programme?

REGINALD. Oh, programme (*HE struggles back to the aisle to buy one.*) Excuse me ... Sorry...

KEITH. (*Patiently and quietly.*) Got change? Good. Thought you'd only have a twenty-pound note ... Why did I take up this kind of work? Why didn't I become an accountant, like my father said? Right, you've found Row F, you've got a programme.

(*The USHERETTE departs. REGINALD starts to struggle back to rejoin his family.*)

KEITH. So can you sit down and stop ruining my life? No, you can't, can you. Because ...

(*EILEEN and WENDY have discovered that there are only two empty seats. They all three cower in them while they debate the question.*)

EILEEN. (*Whispers.*) There's only two!
REGINALD. (*Whispers.*) What?
EILEEN. (*Whispers.*) Seats! Only two!
KEITH. (*Patiently and quietly.*) Something wrong somewhere. So now what do you do? You go right back to square one. Re-examine every shred of evidence.

(*THEY check their ticket stubs.*)

KEITH. The tickets stubs. Good. Do the ticket stubs hold some clue?
REGINALD. (*Whispers.*) G. They're G.
KEITH. Row G. Of course. You ask around to discover if this is Row G.
REGINALD. (*Whispers to HELENA.*) Is this Row G?
KEITH. An inquiry is set in motion.

(HELENA hunts for her ticket stub.)

JOAN. *(Whispers, to HELENA.)* What, dear?
HELENA. *(Whispers, to JOAN.)* Is this Row G?
KEITH. And, good heavens, it's not Row G at all.

(JOAN discovers the letter on the end of the row.)

JOAN. *(Whispers, to HELENA.)* F.
HELENA. *(Whispers, to REGINALD.)* F.
REGINALD. (Whispers.) F?
KEITH. Yes —F.
REGINALD. *(To EILEEN and WENDY.)* F. We're in F.
KEITH. So where's Row G? Row G is where you were before.

(REGINALD and his family struggle back to the aisle.)

REGINALD. *(Whispers, to JOAN and HELENA.)* Extremely sorry...
EILEEN. *(Whispers, likewise.)* Sorry ... Sorry ...

(THEY squeeze into Row G, past QUENTIN and LEE, to the single empty seat.)

REGINALD. *(Whispers, to QUENTIN and LEE.)* Terribly sorry ... Extremely sorry ...
EILEEN. *(Whispers, likewise.)* Double yellow line ...
KEITH. And now things go from bad to worse.
REGINALD. *(Whispers, likewise.)* There's only one!

(REGINALD and his family cower in the single seat as best they can while THEY think about the problem.)

KEITH. Yes, there's only one empty seat in Row G. This is all very much like my own life! But you don't give up. You don't lie down on the floor in the darkness in silent despair. You take counsel among yourselves. You doggedly pursue your investigations.

REGINALD. (*Whispers, to CHARLES.*) Excuse me— are these 15 and 16?

(*CHARLES obligingly gets up and finds the number on the seats.*)

CHARLES. (*Whispers, to REGINALD.*) 15. 15 and 16.

REGINALD. (*Whispers, to CHARLES.*) I think you're in our seats.

CHARLES. (*Whispers.*) In your seats? (*HE feels in his pocket for his ticket stubs.*)

KEITH. You search your files for deeds and contracts.

CHARLES. (*Finds them, and whispers.*) 15 and 16.

REGINALD. (*Whispers.*) 15 and 16? (*Shows him his own ticket stubs.*) 15 and 16.

KEITH. Now what? You fight. You summon lawyers. A feud starts that will be carried on by your families from generation to generation, to claim the lives of grandchildren and great-grandchildren yet unborn. Or else you ask...

REGINALD. (*Whispers, as politely as ever.*) G 15 and 16?

CHARLES. (*Whispers, likewise.*) F 15 and 16.

KEITH. Ah

REGINALD. (*Whispers.*) I think this is G.

KEITH. *I* think it's G.

CHARLES. (*Whispers.*) This is F.

KEITH. I think not, old fruit.

REGINALD. (*Whispers.*) I think that's F.

HELENA. (*Whispers.*) This is F.

CHARLES. (*Whispers.*) That's F?
HELENA. (*Whispers.*) F.
JOAN. (*Whispers.*) F. This is F. We're in F.
QUENTIN. (*Whispers.*) This is G.
BOBBIE. (*Whispers, helpfully.*) This is I. We're in I.

(*A pause, while CHARLES thinks about this.*)

KEITH. The whole nation is now embroiled. What's it to be, then? Civil war?
CHARLES. (*Whispers, to AMANDA.*) We're in the wrong seats, darling.
AMANDA. (*Absorbed in the play, whispers.*) What? Oh ...

(*CHARLES and AMANDA collect up their belongings.*)

KEITH. You see? All it takes is a little goodwill and understanding. And there's another dispute peacefully resolved, without resort to the violence and bloodshed so beloved by playwrights.
CHARLES. (*Whispers, to REGINALD.*) Extremely sorry.
REGINALD. (*Whispers, to CHARLES.*) Terribly sorry.
CHARLES. (*Whispers, to all the four people he has to climb over to reach F 15 and 16.*) Sorry ... Sorry ... Sorry ... Sorry ...
AMANDA. (*Whispers, likewise.*) Sorry ... Sorry ... Sorry ... Sorry ...
KEITH. Now, take your coats off. Make yourselves comfortable ... All right? Wonderful.

(REGINALD and EILEEN are now at last established in G 15 and 16, WENDY in G 14. The audience is now disposed as per illustration # 3 on page 50.]
So that WENDY is sitting next to LEE, who has turned to stare at her with complete absorption.)

KEITH. Meanwhile, out there in my play, forgotten by the world, life goes on.

BOBBIE. *(Turning back to stage.)* Yes, now where were we?

REGINALD. What's all this, then?

EILEEN. Who are all these people?

KEITH. Much has happened since our last visit. Winter has given place to spring. New characters have arrived, new bits of plot have come and gone

QUENTIN. *(Suddenly struck by a terrible suspicion about the events on stage.)* Just a moment ...

KEITH. Oh, now what?

QUENTIN. That's not Roddy. *(Finds a slip of paper in his programme.)* That's the understudy! We've been sitting here all evening watching the understudy!

KEITH. All right? Got it straight? Happy now?

QUENTIN. Oh, this is ridiculous! *(Whispers, to LEE.)* Come on. We'll go and have dinner instead.

(QUENTIN gets up to leave. But LEE remains where he is; HE is so absorbed in WENDY that HE does not notice QUENTIN's departure.)

KEITH. Yes, you go and have dinner, then. Don't want anyone here who's not happy with the arrangements.

LEE. *(Turns belatedly.)* What?

KEITH. Nothing. Forget it. Perfect right to go if he doesn't like the casting. Just so long as he doesn't ...

(Exit QUENTIN, slamming the doors.)

KEITH. ... slam the doors.

(LEE resumes his contemplation of WENDY.)

KEITH. All right. Now all the rest of us have got to concentrate very hard. So we're all going to have to face the front...

EILEEN. I can't take this in. I don't know what's going on. Never catch up now.

KEITH. Don't panic. A little extra coaching, that's all you need.

REGINALD. Half over. I knew this was going to be a disaster.

KEITH. Don't despair. If we all pay attention ...

WENDY. I can't think with everyone staring!

KEITH. No one's staring.

LEE. Oh God, make her turn her head.

WENDY. *(Turns her head, then quickly looks back at the stage.)* He's staring.

KEITH. He won't stare if you don't take any notice of him.

(WENDY sneaks another quick look at LEE.)

KEITH. Look, if you can't behave we'll have to separate you.

REGINALD. *(Becomes aware of LEE's attention to WENDY.)* Oh no. Oh no. I haven't paid fifteen pounds a head for *that*. *(HE insists on changing places with WENDY.)*

WENDY. Now what?

EILEEN. Now where's he off to?

REGINALD. Forty-five pounds, plus drinks and refreshments.

WENDY. (*Standing.*) Oh God, I'm twelve feet tall.

LEE. Oh God, he's twelve feet wide.

KEITH. I'm sorry. But it's for your own good.

REGINALD. Plus a meal.

KEITH. Yes, yes.

REGINALD. Plus getting back and finding the car's been clamped.

EILEEN. *Now* what's he complaining about?

KEITH. Nothing.

WENDY. I hate being *argued* over!

KEITH. Fair enough. So we can all settle down ...

JOAN. (*Looks at CHARLES.*) *I* know where I've seen him! He sits on the wildlife, with Christopher!

KEITH. Yes, never mind about that.

JOAN. Odd—I thought it was the wildlife tonight.

KEITH. It is, it is, but we can't think about our personal problems now. So, let's just recap. (*HE indicates the stage.*) This one's on, those two are in love, the other one's gone off in a huff. Now ...

(*Enter QUENTIN.*)

KEITH. What? What's *he* come back for?

(*Various PEOPLE turn round to watch as QUENTIN returns to his seat.*)

KEITH. Don't all turn round! It's only him!

QUENTIN. (*Whispers, to LEE.*) I thought we were leaving?

(EVERYONE else turns to watch—except LEE, who is trying to see WENDY on the other side of REGINALD, and WENDY, who is trying not to be seen.)

KEITH. Come on, then. Let's get it settled.

QUENTIN. *(Whispers, to LEE.)* I thought we were leaving.

KEITH. Turn round!

WENDY. Turn round!

(LEE suddenly becomes aware that he is being addressed, and turns to face QUENTIN.)

LEE. *(Whispers, to QUENTIN.)* What?

KEITH. He thought you were leaving.

QUENTIN. *(Whispers, to LEE.)* Are we leaving or aren't we?

LEE. *(Whispers, to QUENTIN.)* Oh ...Well...

KEITH. He doesn't want to.

QUENTIN. *(Whispers, to LEE.)* What?

KEITH. He doesn't want to!

WENDY. Yes, leave him alone!

LEE. I'm quite ...

QUENTIN. *(Whispers, to LEE.)* You're what?

KEITH. Hooked. He's hooked.

QUENTIN. *(Whispers, to LEE.)* Hooked?

KEITH. Yes! Hooked! People get hooked on this play, you know. I've seen people hooked.

WENDY. His Dad's as bad as mine.

QUENTIN. *(Whispers, to LEE.)* You mean, you're *enjoying* it?

LEE. *(Whispers, to QUENTIN.)* Well ...You know ...

WENDY. Yes! He's enjoying it!

KEITH. We're all enjoying it!

WENDY. I'm enjoying it!

(SHE gives a sudden laugh. The OTHERS all quickly turn back to the stage.)

AMANDA. What?

JOAN. What?

REGINALD. What?

KEITH. Yes! You see?

QUENTIN. Oh, well—if this is the type of thing you like. *(HE sits down in his seat again.)*

KEITH. Very kind of you. Now. Everyone watching? Everyone listening? Another laugh coming up. Wait for it, wait for it ...

(A laugh from BOBBIE. AMANDA, CHARLES, LEE, and WENDY.)

REGINALD. That was a joke? Fifteen pounds a head for that?

EILEEN. They'll laugh at anything these days.

JOAN. Oh, I see. It's a *comedy*.

HELENA. But why can't they laugh more quietly? It spoils it for everyone else.

KEITH. Not bad. Well done. Quite good. All right, sad bit coming up now.

(A sudden much bigger laugh from everyone except KEITH, REGINALD, and MERRILL, who is still asleep.)

KEITH. What? What's funny about that?

REGINALD. *(Suddenly laughs as well.)* Actually, that *is* quite funny.

QUENTIN. Mildly amusing bit here, I suppose.

CHARLES. I like the joke about the knees.

AMANDA. There's something very comic about the man with the hands.

JOAN. Oh, well, if it's a *comedy* ... (*SHE laughs.*)

HELENA. (*Her smile disappearing.*) No, that's rather sad, when you come to think about it.

(*Another laugh from the same people. Once again REGINALD joins in late.*)

EILEEN. Oh, he's off!

WENDY. Oh God, please don't let him laugh!

REGINALD. (*His whole attitude changing.*) This is very funny!

KEITH. (*Baffled.*) You wouldn't like to explain the joke to me, would you?

(*REGINALD leads the next laugh, and goes on to lead a round of applause. MERRILL wakes up. HE gets to his feet and begins to leave, a satisfied customer.*)

MERRILL. Great play. Great play. What next?

(*BOBBIE sits him down again.*)

KEITH. Well, so much for *her* broken heart. If they laugh at *his* miseries ...

(*Another laugh from everyone except MERRILL, KEITH, and HELENA.*)

KEITH. They're psychopaths!

(*In fact REGINALD continues after all the others have finished.*)

KEITH. Oh dear.

EILEEN. Never stop him now.

KEITH. This is going to be like one of those burglar alarms you can't switch off till the people come back on Monday.

LEE. God, parents!

WENDY. I don't know this man! He's not my father! There was a mix-up at the hospital!

(People begin to watch REGINALD instead of the stage, and laugh at his laughter. EILEEN looks at him with distaste. WENDY hides her face.)

BOBBIE. Oh, someone's enjoying himself!

CHARLES. This is better than the show!

JOAN. Friend of the author, I expect.

HELENA. All these happy families! All out having a good time, being together ...

(SHE weeps.)

KEITH. *(Resignedly.)* Better put his name on the billing ... Turn all the seats round ... Get the reviewers back ... Cast of one—no set—the producer should be happy...

(Suddenly REGINALD stops laughing. HE points at the stage.)

REGINALD. Hold on! Hold on!

(Everyone turns back towards the stage to see what it is.)

REGINALD. That one! That man!

BOBBIE/CHARLES. *(Together.)* Who?

REGINALD. Him! He's told his wife a lie!

JOAN. Oh no!

CHARLES. Well, not a lie, exactly ...

WENDY. Yes—he said he was going to be at the committee meeting!

HELENA. That's right. He did.

CHARLES. Well ...

REGINALD. He's *not* at the committee meeting!

CHARLES. No, but ...

HELENA. He's here!

CHARLES. Yes. Well, yes.

BOBBIE. *Oh* oh! *Oh* oh!

(*Pause. THEY all watch enthralled, apart from MERRILL.who is asleep again.*)

KEITH. Got them.

QUENTIN. (*Absorbed.*) He's going to have to invent something else.

CHARLES. She won't believe *that*.

HELENA. No, she'll believe anything.

AMANDA. I suppose this is all *my* fault, is it?

HELENA. (*Weeps.*) How could she be such a fool?

QUENTIN. In fact he's living with that man who's in the thing at the whatsit.

KEITH. But why now? Why this bit?

JOAN. Oh no! He's not going to jump to conclusions ...?

(*Her voice trails away. THEY all watch, horrified.*)

KEITH. (*Calmly.*) I think he is, you know. He's going to jump to a conclusion ... right ... *now*!

(*The entire audience, even the suddenly awake MERRILL, jumps to its feet. Pause.*)

KEITH. No, he isn't. (*HE gestures them down, like a conductor. THEY all subside, with a sigh.*) Yes, he is! (*HE gestures them up, and up they all spring. Pause.*) No.

(*THEY start to sit.*)

KEITH. Yes!

(*THEY spring up again. Pause.*)

LEE. No, he isn't —it's *her*!
CHARLES. *She's* going to ...
KEITH. Yes!
JOAN. Oh, no!
KEITH. Oh, yes!
BOBBIE. Don't just stand there!
AMANDA. Move!

(*The entire audience begins to move in unison, like a chorus line, to the right.*)

KEITH. Beautiful!
CHARLES. Wait!

(*THEY all stop.*)

REGINALD. Back!

(*THEY all move to the left in unison.*)

KEITH. Perfect!
EILEEN. Stop!

(*THEY all stop.*)

BOBBIE. Kill him, girl, kill him!
KEITH. Up they go!

(*THEY all raise their arms in unison for a karate chop. Pause.*)

AMANDA. (*With a glance at CHARLES.*) That could be him.
CHARLES. (*With a glance at AMANDA.*) That could be her.
LEE. That could be us.
OMNES. (*Except KEITH.*) That could be *me*!
HELENA. And ...
WENDY. No! No!
HELENA. *Down*!
KEITH. Hold it!

(*THEY all bring their hands down in a unison karate chop on HELENA's command, and immediately bounce them up again on KEITH's annulment. THEY wait.*)

BOBBIE. (*With immense relief.*) Oh ... !
QUENTIN. (*Likewise.*) Of course!
HELENA. (*Likewise.*) It was all a silly misunderstanding!
KEITH. You see?

(*THEY all laugh delightedly with relief. THEY turn to each other and put their hands on each other's arm, stranger to stranger, and embrace each other.*)

CHARLES. I was completely convinced!

EILEEN. So was I!

QUENTIN. Even me, for a moment!

REGINALD. You mean, they didn't...? They weren't...?

LEE. No, they were pretending!

REGINALD. Oh, I *see*.

BOBBIE. I was going to kill him!

HELENA. *I* was going to kill him!

AMANDA. Such a relief!

JOAN. They'd never have got the bloodstains out of the upholstery.

MERRILL. Well, it sure beats heart surgery.

KEITH. Bless you, my children, bless you. I love you. Bless you.

BOBBIE. This is just a wonderful party!

QUENTIN. Awfully nice people, when you get to know them.

REGINALD. Very nice class of person here.

LEE. I've met this girl ...

WENDY. I've met this boy ...

JOAN. It's like the war.

EILEEN. You're all thrown together.

AMANDA. You all do your bit.

HELENA. You forget your own problems.

QUENTIN. Just keep your chin up.

CHARLES. Keep smiling.

REGINALD. (*Sings.*) Roll out the barrel ...

OMNES. (*Except KEITH, join in.*) ...We'll have a barrel of fun ...

KEITH. (*Holds up his hand to stop them.*) OK, people! Hold it! Let's not overdo it!

(*The song dies away in laughter and applause.*)

KEITH. It's still only Act One. Let's leave ourselves somewhere to go in Act Two.

BOBBIE. Oh, right! The play! (*SHE turns back to face the stage.*)

KEITH. One last emotional spasm, and you can all go out and have a drink.

OMNES. (*Except KEITH and BOBBIE.*) Hurrah!

BOBBIE. (*Pointing at the stage.*) Oh my God!

AMANDA. What?

QUENTIN. Where?

HELENA. Who?

(*THEY all spin round to face the stage, and gasp. THEY stand transfixed.*)

KEITH. (*Calmly.*) All right? Sorry. Couldn't resist. It all helps the bar sales. Now, one last little laugh ...

(*A moment's pause, then THEY all laugh and sit down.*)

KEITH. Thank you.

(*The scrim comes down, lit by the lights from the stage, where we are sitting, and opaque. The AUDIENCE begins to applaud as it vanishes. As soon as the scrim touches the floor, the stage lights go off and the houselights beyond come up, so that the scrim becomes transparent, and is taken straight out again. The doors are open at the back, and the USHERETTE has taken up her position with the ice cream tray. The audience beyond is now all seated, and applauding politely. Everyone is as disconnected from the strangers around them as when they came in. THEY yawn and stretch, and become ordinary.*)

CHARLES. (*To AMANDA.*) Well ...

QUENTIN. (*To LEE.*) Well ...

EILEEN. (*To WENDY.*) Quite, you know ... I mean, in places.

JOAN. (*To HELENA.*) Yes, so I said to her, 'Forty pounds, and that included delivery and fitting.' She said, 'That is astonishing ...'

(*HELENA blows her nose and wipes her eyes.*)

JOAN. Are you all right?
HELENA. Fine, fine.
JOAN. 'That is utterly astonishing,' she said ...

(*SHE continues the story inaudibly. HELENA opens her handbag and restores her appearance.*)

REGINALD. Well, I don't know, I thought that was quite, you know ...
EILEEN. Yes, I thought it was really quite, well ...
REGINALD. (*To WENDY.*) How about you?
WENDY. (*Inaudibly.*) Yes.
REGINALD. What?
WENDY. (*Embarrassed at raising her voice.*) I said, yes, lovely.
EILEEN. I mean, it's that sort of play, isn't it.
CHARLES. (*To AMANDA.*) All right, quick sprint to the bar?
AMANDA. (*Sotto voce, to CHARLES.*) Wait.
CHARLES. What?
AMANDA. Make sure there's no one I know! (*SHE cautiously surveys the rest of the audience.*)
CHARLES. Oh, right.

(*HE waits good-humouredly. KEITH and QUENTIN stand up to leave.*)

QUENTIN. (*To LEE.*) No, it's a shame. He wrote *one*. What was it called—nine or ten years ago—set in a school or a brothel or somewhere. Never done another one ...

(*KEITH abruptly sits down again.*)

BOBBIE. (*Looks in her programme, to MERRILL.*) Fifteen minutes. You'll just make it there and back. (*To KEITH.*) Oh no! He's taken his shoes off!
MERRILL. Always take my shoes off when I go to bed.

(*BOBBIE stands over him while HE puts them on again.*)

BOBBIE. (*To KEITH.*) Our honeymoon! Day two! Spent our wedding night on Pan Am!

(*KEITH smilingly stands up again to extract himself from this conversation.*)

QUENTIN. (*Shows LEE the programme.*) Not the kind of face you want to see on an author, is it.

(*KEITH sits down again and conceals his face.*)

QUENTIN. But you're extracting some enjoyment from it, are you?
LEE. (*Cautiously.*) Well, I quite liked ... (*LEE searches in his programme.*) You go on. I'll catch you up.
QUENTIN. No hurry—I did order. You quite liked who?

(*HE looks over LEE's shoulder. LEE is distracted by trying to hear what WENDY is doing.*)

REGINALD. (*Stands up, to WENDY and EILEEN.*)
Well, I think we've all earned a choc-ice.

WENDY. (*Inaudibly.*) I don't want one.

REGINALD. What?

WENDY. I said, I don't want one.

EILEEN. (*Baffled.*) Don't want one?

WENDY. *You* have one. I'll stay here.

EILEEN. It's your birthday!

WENDY. (*Covers her face with her hands.*) Oh God!

REGINALD. (*Jerks his head at EILEEN to summon her
and leave WENDY.*) Next year we'll have her birthday treat
on our own ... Don't leave anything of value behind.

(*EILEEN squeezes past WENDY. SHE and REGINALD
then squeeze past QUENTIN and LEE. THEY go to the
USHERETTE to buy their choc-ices. MERRILL is
now standing up, but not moving.*)

BOBBIE. (*To MERRILL.*) Now what?

MERRILL. (*To BOBBIE.*) My foot.

BOBBIE. Your foot?

MERRILL. My left foot. Something damned funny
with my left foot.

(*KEITH bends down and produces a shoe from the floor of
his row.*)

BOBBIE. (*To KEITH.*) Oh, bless you!

(*SHE takes the shoe from KEITH and gives it to
MERRILL, who sits down again to put it on.*)

BOBBIE. (*To KEITH.*) His wife died. You know—on
the brain. Four kids—but where are they when you need
them?

CHARLES. (*To AMANDA.*) Think we might put our heads over the parapet?

(*HE stands up. AMANDA reluctantly follows suit.*)

CHARLES. Yes, I was a bit distracted for the first half-hour or so by the feel of your knee ...

(*HELEN stands up to let them past, and CHARLES sees her properly for the first time.*)

CHARLES. Oh, hello!

HELENA. (*Vaguely, putting her make-up away.*) Hello... Oh, hello...!

CHARLES. I didn't...

HELENA. No. No.

CHARLES. And you've been sitting ...?

HELENA. Here, yes.

CHARLES. Well ... what a surprise!

HELENA. Yes! (*To JOAN.*) Mother, this is—isn't it Mr. Tolly?—Mr. and Mrs. Tolly.

JOAN. (*Stands up and shakes hands with CHARLES.*) Yes, I think we have ...

CHARLES. I think we have ...

JOAN. You're on the wildlife, with Christopher.

CHARLES. That's right.

JOAN. (*To AMANDA, shaking hands.*) But I don't think we've ever actually ...

AMANDA. (*Brightly.*) No. No.

HELENA. (*To AMANDA.*) I think we have, haven't we...? Oh, no, sorry. You're not ... Are you?

AMANDA. (*Smiling.*) No. No. No.

CHARLES. (*Smoothly.*) No, she couldn't make it tonight. Alas.

HELENA. Oh, how sad.

CHARLES. Yes. Are you enjoying it?
HELENA. Wonderful!
CHARLES. Wonderful!
AMANDA. Wonderful!
CHARLES. Anyway, very nice to run into you.

(*HELENA and JOAN begin to move towards the exit. But their way out is blocked by REGINALD and EILEEN, who are still getting change from the USHERETTE.*)

USHERETTE. Nineteen pounds ninety-five ... nineteen pounds ninety-seven ... nineteen pounds ninety-eight ... Hold on ...

(*CHARLES turns back towards AMANDA, all his composure gone.*)

CHARLES. (*Quietly.*) Oh my God! Oh my God!
AMANDA. (*Quietly.*) I knew it! I knew it!
JOAN. (*To HELENA.*) I didn't catch his wife's name.
HELENA. (*Brightly.*) No. No.
JOAN. You didn't catch it either?
HELENA. No. No.
JOAN. Funny—I thought it was Christopher's wildlife tonight?
HELENA. (*Tautly.*) *I* thought it was Christopher's wildlife tonight.
JOAN. Funny.
HELENA. Very funny.
USHERETTE. Nineteen pounds ninety-nine ...Hold on.
REGINALD. Oh, keep the change.

(*REGINALD and EILEEN go out with their choc-ices. JOAN and HELENA follow them.*)

QUENTIN. Who?
LEE. What?
QUENTIN. You quite liked who?
LEE. Oh ... (*Shows QUENTIN a name in the programme.*) Him.
QUENTIN. Him?
LEE. Well, you know ...
QUENTIN. That was the understudy.
LEE. Oh, sorry.

(*QUENTIN turns firmly to lead the way out. LEE, with a last despairing look at WENDY, follows him.*)

QUENTIN. Never mind. I've booked a table afterwards in that little place across the road. I don't know whether you like oysters ...

(*QUENTIN goes out. LEE hesitates in the doorway. CHARLES and AMANDA make their way up the aisle, squabbling quietly. WENDY watches them.*)

AMANDA. We can't just sit there next to them all the way through Act Two!
CHARLES. Well, we can't leave, or they'll think ...
AMANDA. Think what?
CHARLES. Think, you know ...
AMANDA. They think that already!

(*CHARLES and AMANDA go out. WENDY is left looking at LEE, still hesitating in the doorway. SHE turns quickly back to face the front. LEE is emboldened to come back and sit in his original seat.*)

LEE. (*To WENDY, desperately.*) Sorry—can I sort of ask you something?

WENDY. (*Nervously.*) What?

LEE. I, you know, just thought I sort of heard them say it's your birthday.

WENDY. Yes.

LEE. (*Amazed and delighted.*) Fantastic! I mean, coincidence!

WENDY. What, it's not your birthday?

LEE. Yes! Month after next!

WENDY. (*Also amazed and delighted.*) Oh, fantastic!

(*BOBBIE indicates LEE and WENDY to KEITH.*)

BOBBIE. (*Sotto voce, to KEITH.*) Sweet!

(*KEITH smiles and nods. LEE and WENDY do not notice them.*)

LEE. I mean, we could have a, you know, like birthday drink sort of thing, I mean afterwards.

WENDY. Oh, afterwards, well, I've got to have this sort of meal or something with my, you know ...

LEE. Yes, I've got to go off with this ... well, it's the Drama Group...

(*THEY sit in despair.*)

MERRILL. (*Standing up, to BOBBIE.*) OK. Clear for take-off.

BOBBIE. (*To KEITH.*) Would you believe two months ago this old fellow was lying on a hospital floor, clinically dead?

MERRILL. Well, that was one great play, baby girl.

BOBBIE. (*To KEITH.*) He thinks he's through! He'll be back on the floor again when he finds out!

(MERRILL and BOBBIE begin to move extremely slowly towards the doors.)

LEE. Or I mean we could sort of, you know ...
WENDY. What?
LEE. Well ... go now.
WENDY. What, in the middle? You mean, just ...?
LEE. Just sort of, you know ...
WENDY. We can't just... I mean, we can't ...We can't just sort of, you know... I mean ... Come on, quick, then.
BOBBIE. *(To KEITH.)* Who knows, we may be back for Act Two!

(KEITH manages a smile.)

MERRILL. Act Two? Great. Loved it.
BOBBIE. *(To KEITH.)* He loved Act Two!
MERRILL. Lousy ending.
BOBBIE. Oh. You didn't like the ending?
MERRILL. Sounded like you'd still got half the play to come ...

(HE totters slowly out on BOBBIE's arm. KEITH, watched by the USHERETTE, gloomily opens a newspaper, and puts his feet up on the seats in front.)

Curtain

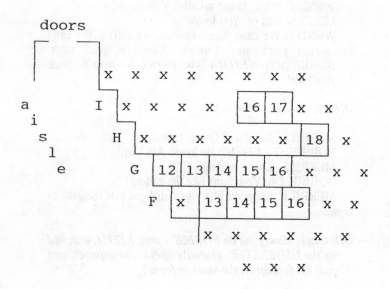

Illustration #1

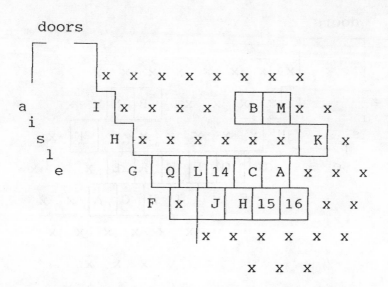

Illustration # 2

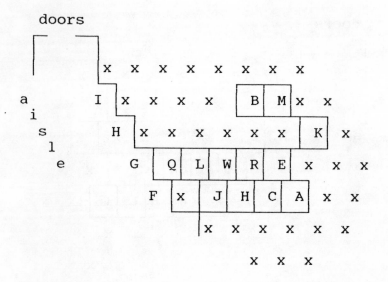

Illustration #3

Other Publications for Your Interest

BENEFACTORS
(LITTLE THEATRE—COMIC DRAMA)
By MICHAEL FRAYN

2 men, 2 women—Interior

Do not expect another *Noises Off*; here the multi-talented Mr. Frayn has more on his mind than Just Plain Fun. *Benefactors*, a long-running Broadway and London hit, is about doing good and do-gooding (not the same) and about the way the world changes outside your control just when you are trying to change it yourself. The story concerns an architect who has the sixties notion that if you give people good environments they will be good people. But, given a South London development to design, he is forced by town planners to go for a high-rise, characterless scheme. No sooner does he begin to believe in this scheme than the fashion for high rises goes bust. ". . . one of the subtlest plays Broadway has seen in years, by one of the most extraordinary writers of the English-speaking theater . . . more political than most political plays, more intimate than most intimate plays and wiser than almost any play around today."—Newsweek. ". . . a fine . . . very good play . . . A Christmas present for theatergoers."—WABC-TV. ". . . a high point of the theater season . . . rare wit and intelligence."—Wall Street Journal. ". . . fascinating and astonishing play . . ."—N.Y. Daily News. ". . . dazzling and devastating play . . ."—N.Y. Times. ". . . a tour de force . . . simultaneously compelling and alienating . . ."—Christian Science Monitor. (#3980)

PACK OF LIES
(LITTLE THEATRE—DRAMA)
By HUGH WHITEMORE

3 men, 5 women—Combination interior

Bob and Barbara Jackson are a nice middle-aged English couple. Their best friends are their neighbors, Helen and Peter Kroger, who are Canadian. All is blissful in the protected, contained little world of the Jacksons; until, that is, a detective from Scotland Yard asks if his organization may use the Jackson's house as an observation station to try and foil a Soviet spy ring operating in the area. Being Good Citizens the Jacksons oblige, though they become progressively more and more put out as Scotland Yard's demands on them increase. They are really put to the test when the detective reveals to them that the spies are, in fact, their best friends the Krogers. Scotland Yard asks the Jacksons to cooperate with them to trap the spies, which really puts the Jacksons on the horns of a dilemma. Do they have the right to "betray" their friends? "This is a play about the morality of lying, not the theatrics of espionage, and, in Mr. Whitemore's view, lying is a virulent disease that saps patriots and traitors alike of their humanity."—N.Y. Times. "A crackling melodrama."—Wall St. Journal. "Absolutely engrossing . . . an evening of dynamic theatre."—N.Y. Post. "A superior British drama."—Chr. Sci. Mon. (#18154)